Contents

Words in the glossary appear in **bold** type the first time they are used in the text.

FUEL OF LIFE

We live in a world that runs on **fossil fuels** such as oil, coal, and natural gas. Fossil fuels are found within Earth and can be used to create energy. We power our cars, heat our homes, and make products such as plastic with fossil fuels. These fuels aren't renewable, which means there's a limited supply of them.

As we search for new sources of energy, the ways we find fossil fuels have advanced as well. Man's search for fossil fuels such as natural gas can often have terrible consequences for the people and animals that live where these natural resources are found.

First Find

Natural gas was first found as people drilled for oil and other fossil fuels. Many **deposits** of oil, coal, and natural gas would be found together because all fossil fuels are made by the same process: decaying plants and animals, put under intense pressure over a long period of time.

oil wells

HABITAT HAVOC

FRACKING

By Ryan Nagelhout

Gareth Stevens

Please visit our website, www.garethstevens.com. For a free color catalog of all our high-quality books, call toll free 1-800-542-2595 or fax 1-877-542-2596.

Library of Congress Cataloging-in-Publication Data

Nagelhout, Ryan.
Fracking / by Ryan Nagelhout.
 p. cm. — (Habitat havoc)
Includes index.
ISBN 978-1-4339-9855-3 (pbk.)
ISBN 978-1-4339-9856-0 (6-pack)
ISBN 978-1-4339-9919-2 (library binding)
1. I. Nagelhout, Ryan. II. Title.
TD195.G3 C66 2014
622.3381—dc23

First Edition

Published in 2014 by
Gareth Stevens Publishing
111 East 14th Street, Suite 349
New York, NY 10003

Copyright © 2014 Gareth Stevens Publishing

Designer: Andrea Davison-Bartolotta
Editor: Kristen Rajczak

Photo credits: Cover, p. 1 (main image), 20–21 (background), 29 Robert Nickelsberg/Getty Images; cover, pp. 1–32 (red banner) Amgun/Shutterstock.com; cover, back cover, pp. 1–32 (background) Eky Studio/ Shutterstock.com; cover, back cover, p. 1 (border) Redshinestudio/Shutterstock.com; pp. 2–32 (black border) Alex Gontar/Shutterstock.com; pp. 4, 6 (shale), 9 (map), 17 (main) iStockphoto/Thinkstock; p. 5 MCT/ MCT via Getty Images; p. 7 (inset) roccomontoya/iStock vectors/Getty Images; p. 7 (background) Calin Tatu/Shutterstock.com; pp. 9 (background), 13 Mladen Antonov/AFP/Getty Images; p. 11 Glynnis Jones/ Shutterstock.com; p. 12 Jupiterimages/Comstock/Thinkstock; pp. 14, 15 Jason Janik/Bloomberg via Getty Images; p. 17 (inset) Laurie Barr/Shutterstock.com; pp. 18–19, 21 (water) Katie Orlinsky/Getty Images; p. 21 (condor) kojihirano/Shutterstock.com; pp. 22–23 Julia Schmalz/Bloomberg via Getty Images; p. 23 (inset) Adam Ziaja/Shutterstock.com; p. 24 Lynn Johnson/National Geographic/Getty Images; p. 25 Patrick T. Fallon/Bloomberg via Getty Images; p. 27 Rich Lasalle/The Image Bank/Getty Images.

Printed in the United States of America

CPSIA compliance information: Batch #CW14GS: For further information contact Gareth Stevens, New York, New York at 1-800-542-2595.

Natural gas is a clean-burning fossil fuel. It's generally less harmful to the environment than other fossil fuels.

WHAT IS FRACKING?

It's **estimated** that more than 25 percent of energy use in the United States is powered by natural gas. That's expected to rise as more companies begin **hydraulic fracturing**, or fracking.

Fracking is a process that brings natural gas trapped in rocks deep underground to Earth's surface. A well is drilled straight down into a layer of rock called shale. Then, the drill is turned, and a tunnel is made **horizontally** through the shale. Next, a **solution** of water, sand, and other chemicals is pumped through the tunnel at a high speed. The solution cracks, or fractures, the shale, freeing the natural gas to flow to the surface.

shale

Shale Plays

Shale is a rock made after mud is subjected to pressure and heat over a long period of time. It breaks into thin pieces with sharp edges. Shale can be many colors, but black shale is made from the animal and plant material that also turns into fossil fuels. An area of the rock where shale gas is found is called a play.

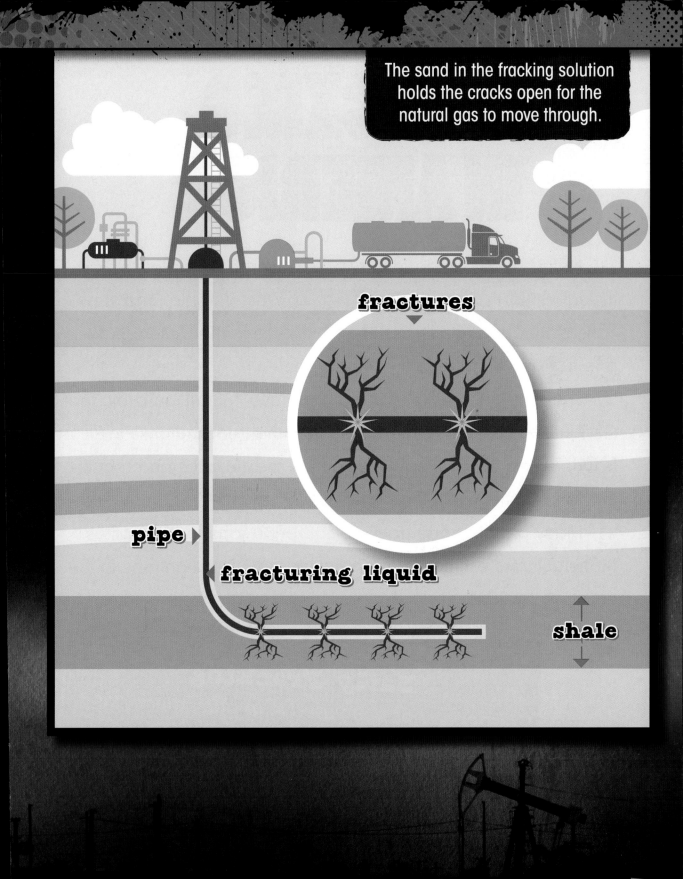

The sand in the fracking solution holds the cracks open for the natural gas to move through.

fractures

pipe

fracturing liquid

shale

FRACKING IN AMERICA

Natural gas can be found in over two dozen states, including North Dakota, Pennsylvania, West Virginia, and New York. Natural gas drilling is huge business in the United States, and fracking has made it even bigger.

The United States is estimated to have 482 trillion cubic feet (13.7 trillion cu m) of shale gas now within reach, thanks to fracking. This could supply the country for decades and reduce the use of other fossil fuels around the nation.

Many people hope fracking can bring jobs to their states. Manufacturers estimate fracking could add 1 million jobs to the economy by 2025.

Early Fracking

Fracking has been used in oil and natural gas wells since the 1940s. Fracking solutions were pumped into **vertical** wells to break through the shale. Machinery developed in the last 2 decades has made it even more useful for directional, or horizontal, drilling. This lets energy companies reach gas in a much larger area.

Shale plays can be found all over the United States. Energy companies see them as an untapped resource that could decrease the country's dependence on fossil fuels from overseas.

shale plays

THE DILEMMA

Not much is known about the impact fracking can have on the environment. The fluid pumped into wells uses chemicals that can harm plants and animals. Fracking wastewater is often put back into lakes and rivers—and some say it shouldn't be. People have started to get sick near fracking wells, and accidents can harm the air, land, and water supply.

Many people want to be careful and study the effects of fracking. Others don't want to hurt growing businesses and keep landowners from making money. Some believe the need for clean energy from natural gas outweighs possible harm fracking may cause.

Marcellus Shale

One of the largest natural gas deposits in the world is under a rock formation called the Marcellus Shale, which stretches across New York and into Pennsylvania and West Virginia. Since 2008, fracking hasn't been allowed in New York. Its government wants to study fracking in other states. In 2013, the state assembly voted to extend the ban until 2015.

People in favor of and against fracking often hold protests.

THE WASTEWATER

Every year, energy companies pump millions of gallons of fracking fluid thousands of feet into the ground. About 70 percent of that solution comes back to the surface, and is then called brine, wastewater, or flowback. It's very salty and full of chemicals and substances from deep within Earth, like uranium and radium.

Depending on state rules, the flowback may be stored for reuse. Some states put it in large open areas called frack ponds. There, brine can evaporate while sitting in these plastic-lined pits. Flowback may also be stored underground.

Don't Drink the Water

In 2005, an energy bill was passed that made fracking companies **exempt** from the Safe Drinking Water Act, which sets standards for drinking water quality. They also don't have to tell what chemicals are in fracking fluid. It's mostly unknown what's in wastewater, too, since it depends on the area being fracked.

Where and how flowback is stored or disposed of is one of the major issues **environmentalists** have with fracking. Many frack ponds lie uncovered and can grow bad-smelling bacteria.

DANGER **DANGER**
RESTRICTED AREA
WATER HAZARD

The dirty, gray wastewater from fracking has many ways of entering the environment. Spills are a regular problem at frack ponds. The plastic pipes leading from wells to ponds crack and leak wastewater into the ground, where animals can drink at puddles. So do the cement and steel casings at the top of well openings. Fracking fluid or flowback can also get into the water supplies when spilled or dumped into rivers and streams.

However it happens, fracking introduces hundreds of chemicals and other substances into the water and soil. Some can cause illness and death.

Fracking Hazards

Energy companies have reported thousands of accidents at well sites a year, including equipment failures, explosions, pollution, and other environmental risks. Residents living nearby often aren't told about these risks unless they complain about smells or illness. Many landowners who sell **mineral rights** to companies don't know the risks they're taking.

DANGER
NO SMOKING

Many fracking companies send flowback to water treatment plants to be cleaned and used again, or prepared for disposal. Here, a worker releases the wastewater carried by trucks into the treatment plant.

THE FRESHWATER

Fracking wells often go through **aquifers**, or places where groundwater can be found. Brine isn't supposed to reach these aquifers, but it commonly does, and then it makes its way into the water supply.

Many water treatment plants don't want to treat the brine. It's hard to do, and many don't have a way to clean the extremely salty water. So, companies often have to ship the wastewater long distances for treatment. Nonetheless, people don't want even treated flowback returned to their drinking water.

Taking thousands of gallons of water out of lakes and rivers for fracking also hurts **habitats** even before the water gets back into the environment.

Safe Drinking Water?

In 2013, Colorado governor and fracking supporter John Hickenlooper told a US Senate committee that he once drank fracking fluid. "I'm still alive," he said. An executive at an energy company called Halliburton once drank fracking fluid during a 2011 speech, but his company's website later said the fluid shouldn't be considered drinkable.

aquifer layer

While the aquifer rock layer works as a natural filter, it doesn't help make the flowback from fracking fluid safer. The wells and fractures allow for more chemicals and minerals to get through the aquifer than could if fracking hadn't occurred.

water treatment plant

THE LIVESTOCK

Where fracking occurs, animals around the drill sites have died or gotten very sick. A study found that 17 cows in Louisiana died within an hour of being exposed to fracking fluid.

For one farmer, cows died shortly after he let them drink from a creek believed to be polluted by brine. The cows he kept away from the creek all survived.

Many farmers have talked to the media about dying horses, cows, and other animals. However, scientists have been unable to directly link fracking to illnesses because it's hard to find out what is in both fracking fluid and flowback.

Fracking Cows

Cows that die on farms aren't used for steaks or hamburgers people eat. But many are turned into food for chickens and pigs that are eaten by people. Some people worry that toxic effects from fracking could make their way into the food supply in this way. Many environmentalists say the cows' health problems are a warning sign about the impact of fracking.

Some animals that live
near fracking sites stop
being able to have babies.

19

In Pennsylvania, farm owners who allowed fracking nearby saw their pets and livestock suddenly die. Dogs seen drinking standing water died just days later of mysterious causes. Tests performed on these animals have found heavy metal poisoning, liver damage, and other serious problems.

Farms that used to win awards for animals began seeing puppies born without hair, or worse, dead. But no one knew why or where the toxic chemicals in their blood came from! Similar problems have been discovered with animals in North Dakota and other places where fracking takes place.

polluted water

Many people suspect fracking chemicals are hurting their animals.

Endangered Animals

Environmental activists worry that fracking activities can harm the populations of endangered **species**, or animals close to dying out altogether. In California alone, fracking activity in six different counties is estimated to impact almost 100 different species such as California condors, San Joaquin kit foxes, and blunt-nosed leopard lizards.

California condor

THE ROADS

Building fracking wells means big trucks need to reach remote places. Trucks carrying supplies can make more than 200 trips back and forth per day while fracking is taking place. That equals a lot of roads, which is good business for construction companies. Winding roads leading from well to well make traveling easy for companies engaged in fracking.

However, these roads disrupt thousands of acres of land previously untouched by human development. People living in rural areas face more air pollution from increased traffic. For animals, these roads can **fragment** habitats and make it difficult for animals to find food and stay away from people.

A Lesser Threat?

Some people say they support fracking because other companies could use the land for more dangerous things. Long-wall coal mining, for example, has diggers removing a long strip of coal from underground and letting the earth above it fall in when mining is finished. Long-wall mining can change entire landscapes.

modern coal mine

Camptown, Pennsylvania, is home to this natural gas production site, which used to look like the beautiful rolling hills and forests surrounding it.

HUMAN HABITATS

People may be the creatures doing the fracking, but they may be doing as much damage to their own habitat as they're doing to other creatures' habitats. There are many horror stories about blisters, bleeding, and other illnesses that developed in people living near wells. Dizziness, shortness of breath, and kidney and lung problems are among the complaints of these residents.

Few long-term studies have been done about the dangers of fracking. Profits made from selling mineral rights have driven many people to allow drilling nearby without knowing what can happen to their land and health.

signs for an oil rig near one for a wildlife refuge

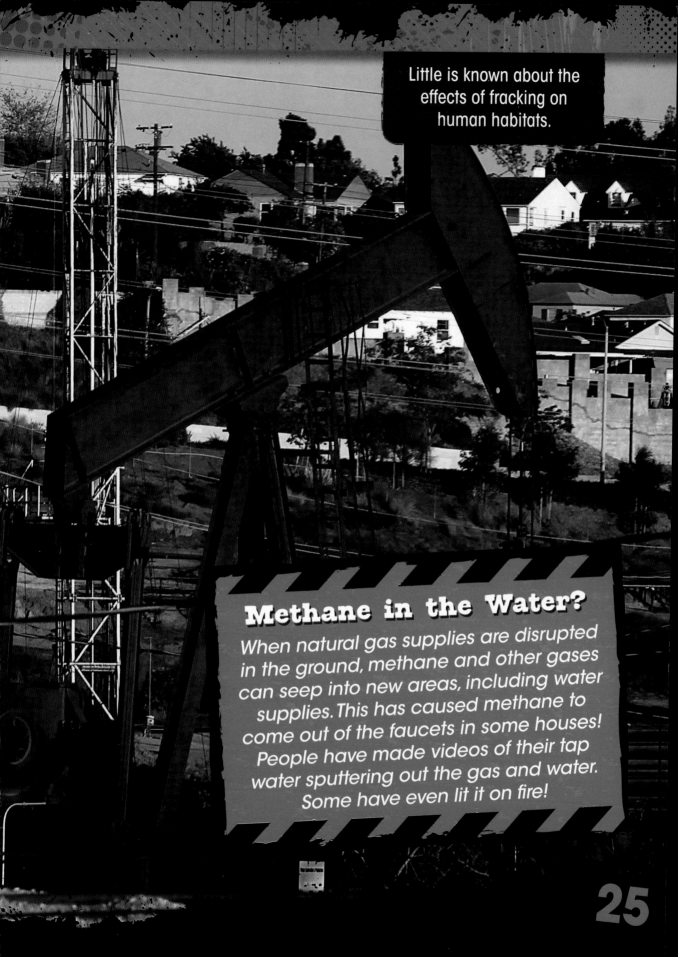

Little is known about the effects of fracking on human habitats.

Methane in the Water?

When natural gas supplies are disrupted in the ground, methane and other gases can seep into new areas, including water supplies. This has caused methane to come out of the faucets in some houses! People have made videos of their tap water sputtering out the gas and water. Some have even lit it on fire!

FRACKING AROUND THE WORLD

Fracking is hotly contested in the United States, but other countries are debating hydraulic fracturing as well.

Poland is beginning to explore fracking in its shale deposits, but protected species nearby have slowed their progress. In Australia, fracking is a booming business, but many people are beginning to worry about its effect on the water and land. Parts of western Canada have embraced fracking at a record pace, but the more populated eastern regions are wary of possible dangers.

Fracking is banned in France, where government officials say they won't harvest shale gas until a safer alternative is found.

China

China gets 4 percent of its energy from natural gas. With the help of fracking, the Chinese hope to double their natural gas percentage by 2015. However, the nation has had trouble accessing the natural gas in its shale deposits due to a lack of water and technology near shale plays.

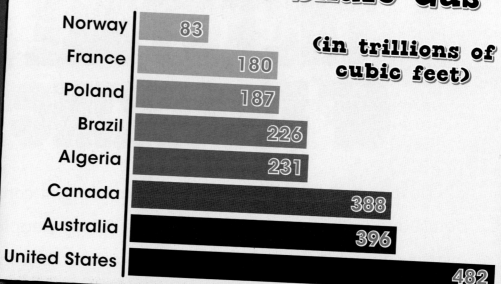

Recoverable Shale Gas

(in trillions of cubic feet)

Norway	83
France	180
Poland	187
Brazil	226
Algeria	231
Canada	388
Australia	396
United States	482

Many nations are exploring hydraulic fracking to access their shale gas, but, as in the United States, environmentalists are worried about the effects.

THE FUTURE OF FRACKING

Despite the dangers of hydraulic fracturing, it continues to be used to take natural gas out of Earth. Many people hope energy companies will tell the public more about what they're putting into the ground and better protect water supplies and animals that live near fracking wells.

Others want the government to closely watch drilling companies to make sure they don't permanently damage the environment. President Barack Obama has already forced companies to share the kinds of chemicals they use on public lands. Still, there are many other ways to protect the environment and make sure we don't wreak havoc on animal habitats—especially our own.

Well Watching

As people debate the dangers of fracking, thousands of wells are drilled and fracked each year. Some estimate over 2,500 new wells a year will be drilled in the Marcellus Shale in Pennsylvania alone, with an expected total of 100,000 wells built over the next few decades.

In 2012, construction of a long pipeline began in Mifflin Township, Pennsylvania. It will transport millions of gallons of water used in fracking.

Glossary

aquifer: a layer of rock, sand, or gravel where water is found

deposit: a gathering of a natural resource

environmentalist: a person who wants to protect the environment

estimate: to make a guess based on facts

exempt: excused

fossil fuel: decayed plant and animal matter such as coal, oil, and natural gas used for energy

fragment: to break apart, or separate

habitat: a place where an animal lives

horizontally: following the same direction as the horizon; sideways

hydraulic fracturing: sending water, sand, and other chemicals into the ground at a high speed to break up rocks

mineral rights: claims to the natural resources under the ground that landowners sell to energy companies

solution: a liquid that has something dissolved in it

species: a group of animals that are all of the same kind

vertical: straight up and down

For More Information

Books

Hillstrom, Kevin. *Fracking*. Detroit, MI: Lucent Books, 2013.

Squire, Ann O. *Hydrofracking: The Process That Has Changed America's Energy Needs*. New York, NY: Children's Press, 2013.

Websites

How Hydraulic Fracking Works
www.howstuffworks.com/environmental/energy/hydraulic-fracking.htm
Read in detail about how natural gas is released from deep within Earth by fracking.

NaturalGas.org
www.naturalgas.org/overview/background.asp
Find out more about natural gas and why it's important.

What is shale gas and why is it important?
www.eia.gov/energy_in_brief/article/about_shale_gas.cfm
Find out more about shale gas at this government site.

Publisher's note to educators and parents: Our editors have carefully reviewed these websites to ensure that they are suitable for students. Many websites change frequently, however, and we cannot guarantee that a site's future contents will continue to meet our high standards of quality and educational value. Be advised that students should be closely supervised whenever they access the Internet.

Index